Fri

WYOMING

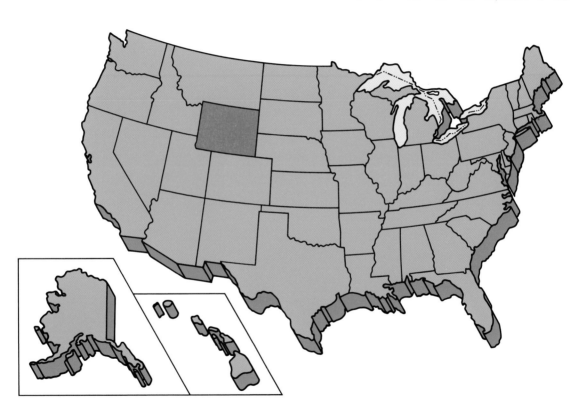

WYOMING

Carlienne Frisch

Lerner Publications Company

LIBRARY OF CONGRESS
CATALOGING-IN-PUBLICATION DATA
Frisch, Carlienne.
    Wyoming / Carlienne Frisch.
        p. cm. — (Hello U.S.A.)
    Includes index.
    Summary: Introduces Wyoming's geography, history, and the ways in which its citizens work and live.
    ISBN 0-8225-2736-7 (lib. bdg.)
    1. Wyoming—Juvenile literature. 2. Wyoming—Geography—Juvenile literature.
[1. Wyoming.] I. Title. II. Series.
F761.3.F75 1994
978.7—dc20   93-23098
                                       CIP
                                        AC

Manufactured in the United States of America

1 2 3 4 5 6 – I/JR – 99 98 97 96 95 94

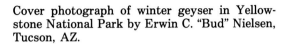

Cover photograph of winter geyser in Yellowstone National Park by Erwin C. "Bud" Nielsen, Tucson, AZ.

The glossary that begins on page 68 gives definitions of words shown in **bold type** in the text.

This book is printed on acid-free, recyclable paper.

CONTENTS

A statue of Esther Morris, the country's first female judge, stands outside Wyoming's state capitol in Cheyenne.

Did You Know . . . ?

☐ In 1869 women in Wyoming became the first females in the nation to be able to vote and to hold public office. Wyomingites elected the nation's first female judge (1870), the first female state legislator (1911), and the first female governor (1925). For these milestones, Wyoming is known as the Equality State.

☐ With about 453,000 people, the entire state of Wyoming has fewer residents than many U.S. cities.

☐ In 1872 Yellowstone National Park in Wyoming became the world's first national park.

☐ Wyoming is famous for its rodeos. But cowboys in the state also compete in a winter event known as a sno-d-o. Here, cowboys on snowmobiles race to rope an iron cow that is pulled across the snow by another snowmobile.

☐ Black Thunder in eastern Wyoming is the largest coal mine in the Americas. Workers at the site dig up about a ton of coal per second. After a day's work, that's enough to fill a train that is 8 miles (13 kilometers) long!

The sun rises over the mountains in western Wyoming *(below)*. Unusual rock formations *(facing page)* jut from the ground in central and eastern Wyoming, where much of the land is flat *(right)*.

8

A Trip
Around the State

The tenth largest state in the country, Wyoming is one of six Rocky Mountain states located in the western United States. Wyoming stretches from Idaho and Utah on the west to South Dakota and Nebraska on the east. Montana is Wyoming's northern neighbor. Colorado and a corner of Utah border Wyoming on the south.

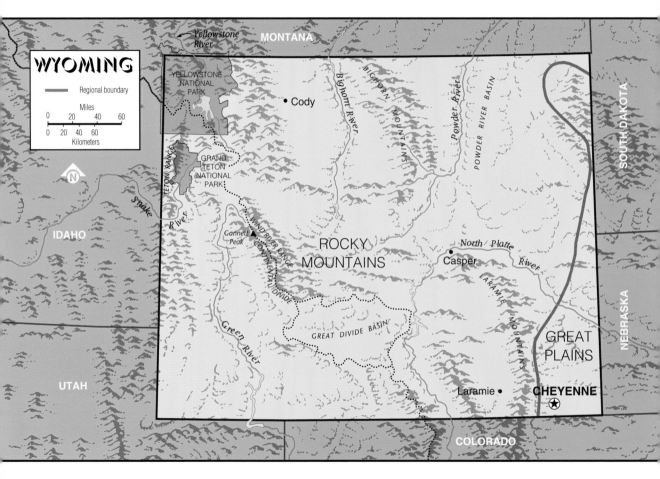

WYOMING

Regional boundary

Miles
0   20   40   60

Kilometers
0 20 40 60

N

MONTANA

Yellowstone River

YELLOWSTONE NATIONAL PARK

• Cody

Bighorn River

BIGHORN MOUNTAINS

Powder River

POWDER RIVER BASIN

GRAND TETON NATIONAL PARK

TETON RANGE

Snake River

Gannett Peak ▲

WIND RIVER RANGE

CONTINENTAL DIVIDE

ROCKY MOUNTAINS

North Platte River

• Casper

LARAMIE MOUNTAINS

IDAHO

Green River

GREAT DIVIDE BASIN

UTAH

Laramie •

CHEYENNE ★

GREAT PLAINS

COLORADO

SOUTH DAKOTA

NEBRASKA

Wyoming takes its name from *meche-weami-ing,* an Indian phrase that means "big river flats" or "on the big plains." The phrase refers to Wyoming's Great Plains—one of the state's two major land regions. A vast area of grassland, the Great Plains region spreads across eastern Wyoming. In the central part of the state, the plains meet the Rocky Mountains (or Rockies), which run north to south and cover much of central and western Wyoming.

Wyoming's Great Plains region is part of a flat, grassy **plateau** (highland) that stretches from Canada to Texas. The mountainous Black Hills of South Dakota spill onto the northeastern corner of Wyoming's plains. Long ridges

Devils Tower, a tall column of volcanic rock, rises in northeastern Wyoming.

and low, steep hills also break up the flat land. Cattle graze on the region's rich variety of grasses.

11

The Rocky Mountain region of Wyoming is part of a large mountain system that runs all the way from Alaska to New Mexico. In the Wind River Range, Wyoming's highest point—Gannett Peak—reaches 13,804 feet (4,207 meters). Other major ranges include the Teton Range and the Bighorn and the Laramie mountains.

Some of these mountain ranges are separated by broad, dry valleys called **basins**. The basins receive so little rain they are sometimes considered deserts. Cattle and sheep are raised in the basins. They graze on the short grasses, sagebrush, and other small plants that don't need a lot of water to grow.

Although much of Wyoming is

With its red rock, the southern part of the Great Divide Basin is sometimes called the Red Desert.

The Lower Falls of the Yellowstone River drop 308 feet (94 meters)—almost twice as far as New York's Niagara Falls.

very dry, the state is famous for snow-fed waterways such as the fast-flowing Yellowstone River. This waterway has carved out a spectacular canyon in Yellowstone National Park in northwestern Wyoming. Other important rivers are the Snake, Green, Bighorn, Powder, and North Platte.

Rivers in Wyoming flow to either the Atlantic Ocean or the Pacific Ocean, depending on which side of the **Continental Divide** they lie. Following a line of Rocky Mountain peaks, the divide cuts through Wyoming from its northwestern corner to the south central part of the state. The rivers on the east side of the divide flow toward the Atlantic. Those on the west flow toward the Pacific.

13

Snow covers most of Wyoming in the winter *(above)*. **Each spring, meadows come alive with Indian paintbrush** *(facing page)* **and other wildflowers.**

14

In general the state's four seasons are cool and dry. The Great Plains are usually warmer and milder than the mountains, where temperatures can drop below freezing even in the summer. January temperatures in the northwestern mountains average an icy 12° F (–11° C). On the Great Plains, the city of Casper averages a more comfortable 22° F (–6° C). The average July temperature in the northwest is 59° F (15° C), while Casper enjoys 71° F (22° C).

Most of Wyoming's **precipitation** (rain and melted snow) falls in the Rockies. Each year the mountains receive about 50 inches (127 centimeters) of rain, while some basin areas get as little as 5 inches (13 cm). In the winter, about 260 inches (660 cm) of snow cover the slopes. In contrast the basins get only 15 inches (38 cm) of snow each year.

Like the weather, the state's plants vary with the elevation, or height, of the land. Indian paintbrush, forget-me-nots, and other wildflowers color the mountainsides each spring. Mosses, lichens, and evergreen trees such as the lodgepole pine and Douglas fir also grow in the high forests.

Strong winds that tend to blow in only one direction force tree branches in some parts of Wyoming to grow in that same direction.

Aspens and other broad-leaved trees appear at lower elevations. More than 150 kinds of grasses, such as bluegrass and redtop, thrive in the Great Plains region. Greasewood shrubs, yuccas, cactuses, and other plants that need little water grow in the driest areas of the state.

Bison, or buffalo, once numbered in the millions on the Great Plains. In Wyoming only a few herds survive, mostly in Yellowstone National Park. The world's largest elk herds spend each winter in the National Elk Refuge at the base of the Tetons.

Grizzly bears share high wilderness areas with black bears, lynxes, and mountain lions. Pronghorn antelope and mule deer graze in the basins and on the Great Plains. Some people even look for a creature called a jackalope—a legendary rabbit said to have the horns of an antelope!

Elk *(above)*, **mountain bluebird** *(bottom right)*, **wild horses** *(top right)*

Wyoming's Story

More than 11,000 years ago, hunters came to what is now Wyoming in search of prey. In the mountains, the hunters found elk and mountain sheep. On the plains roamed bison and woolly mammoths.

To kill their prey, hunters drove the animals over cliffs or into sand pits. Lying wounded on the ground or stuck in the sand, the animals could be easily killed with arrows or spears. People ate the animals' meat and used the skins for clothing and shelter. Bones and horns were made into tools.

Some people who came to present-day Wyoming also fished in mountain streams. Those who lived in the basins gathered roots, nuts, and seeds and hunted lizards, squirrels, and rabbits.

By 1700 groups of American Indians, or Native Americans, were living throughout much of what is now Wyoming. These groups included the Crow, the Shoshone, and other descendants of the early hunters and gatherers. Over time the Cheyenne, Arapaho, Lakota (also called Sioux), and other groups of Plains Indians came to what is now Wyoming from the east. These newcomers pushed the Crow and the Shoshone from the Great Plains into the Rocky Mountain region.

Plains Indian hunters wore snowshoes to track their prey through deep snow.

19

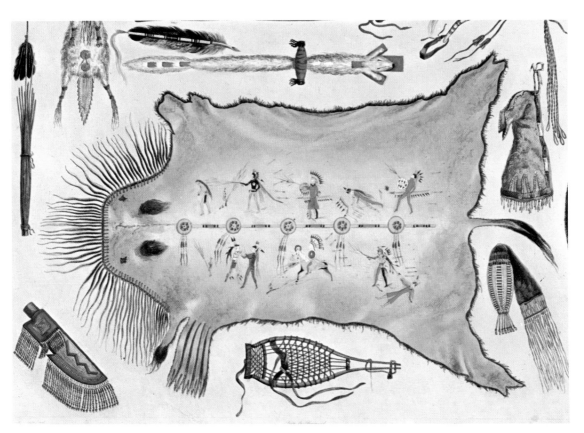

Native Americans painted stories about their lives on buffalo hides *(above).* **Animal skins were used for many things, including clothing and tepee coverings** *(facing page).*

During the summer, the Plains Indians left their villages in search of bison. While on the hunt, the hunters lived in tepees, which were easy to put up and take down. In the autumn, the Indians packed up their tepees and brought the yearly supply of meat back to their villages.

In the early 1700s, horses were brought north into what is now Wyoming from Spanish settlements far to the south. On horseback, the Plains Indians could travel farther from their villages and kill more bison than they could on foot. Many Indians gave up village life to hunt bison year-round.

About 10,000 Indians lived in what is now Wyoming in the mid-1700s, when Europeans first arrived in the region to search for fur-bearing animals. At that time, most of what is now Wyoming was part of the Louisiana Territory, a vast region between the Mississippi River and the Rocky Mountains. France claimed the territory until 1803, when the United States bought the land in a deal called the Louisiana Purchase.

U.S. president Thomas Jefferson sent explorers Meriwether Lewis and William Clark to map the territory in 1804. Although they never entered what is now Wyoming, the two men came back with tales of the West's plentiful wildlife.

Because of these stories, trappers and traders from the eastern United States and from Canada headed toward the Rockies. The adventurers hoped to get rich trapping beavers, whose furs were sold at very high prices in Europe to be made into stylish hats.

In 1825 fur trader William Ashley held the first annual trappers' gathering on the Green River in what is now western Wyoming. Every summer for the next 15 years, trappers came to this same place on the same date. The trappers, also called mountain men, told stories, played games, and exchanged furs with traders for food, weapons, and other supplies.

A mountain man checks his animal traps.

In 1834 fur traders William Sublette and Robert Campbell built Fort William, the first permanent white settlement in what is now Wyoming. In the next few years, more trading posts were built. But by the early 1840s, mountain men had trapped most of the beavers in the region, and beaver hats were going out of style in Europe. As a result, many trappers and traders left what is now Wyoming.

The trading posts they left behind became important supply stations for pioneers, who began crossing Wyoming in the 1840s. Many of these travelers, who came from crowded areas in the eastern United States, were looking for land to farm. Pioneers headed west on the California Trail, the Oregon Trail, and the Mormon Trail. These routes all crossed the Rockies through South Pass—a break in the mountains in what is now southwestern Wyoming.

In 1848 gold was discovered in California, and the gold rush was on. At its peak in 1850, more than 50,000 gold seekers made the long and difficult trip across what is now Wyoming on their way to the gold fields. Over time so many wagons rolled across the land that their wheels formed waist-deep ruts in the earth.

Pioneer wagon trains *(above)* traveled about 8 miles (13 kilometers) each day. The ruts left in the earth by heavy wagon wheels *(inset)* can still be seen in eastern Wyoming.

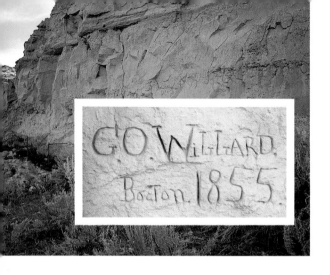

Thousands of pioneers on the Oregon Trail carved their names *(inset)* **into some of Wyoming's rocky hills** *(left).*

Most of the pioneer trails across the Great Plains followed rivers. Some of the waterways dried up during the summer, when most pioneers made the journey west. Travelers could usually carry enough water for themselves, but sometimes the oxen that pulled the wagons died of thirst.

Many oxen couldn't find enough grass to eat along the trail and starved to death. To lighten the load for the tired and hungry animals, pioneers often abandoned their belongings on the trail or left them behind at trading posts. Because the region was so dry, very few people settled in what is now Wyoming.

As they drove their wagons across Indian hunting grounds, the pioneers killed wild game for food, leaving fewer animals for the Indians to hunt. The pioneers'

Members of a wagon train pose for a picture at South Pass, where pioneers crossed the Rockies.

cooking fires sometimes blazed out of control and quickly burned up the dry prairie grasses nearby, which bison needed to survive. The pioneers also carried smallpox and other deadly diseases to which the Indians had never before been exposed. Thousands of Indians caught these illnesses, and many died.

All these changes threatened the Indians and their way of life. Angered, they sometimes attacked wagon trains. To protect pioneers traveling along the Oregon Trail, the U.S. government bought the trading post at Fort William and turned it into a military site called Fort Laramie. U.S. soldiers at the fort made sure pioneers could travel safely.

Tensions rose between pioneers and Indians after gold was discovered in Montana in the early 1860s. Gold seekers followed a new route called the Bozeman Trail. This path crossed Indian hunting grounds in what is now north central Wyoming. Groups of Sioux, led by Red Cloud, attacked many wagon trains on this trail. In response the U.S. government built even more forts and sent additional soldiers to the area.

Finally, after many battles, the U.S. government and Sioux leaders signed a peace **treaty** in 1868. The U.S. government agreed to give up its forts and to set aside **reservations,** or areas of land just for the Indians. In exchange the Indians agreed to allow a new kind of trail to be built—this one for trains.

Pioneers and Indians fought so many battles along the Bozeman Trail that it was closed only a few years after it opened.

The Union Pacific Railroad had already begun to lay tracks across what is now southern Wyoming. Many of the railroad workers were **immigrants** who came from China. The Union Pacific also hired Irish and Scandinavian laborers, as well as many Latinos.

The railroad attracted thousands of new settlers to what is now Wyoming. Those who didn't lay tracks had jobs mining coal, which was used to fuel the trains. Cities and towns such as Cheyenne and Laramie sprang up almost overnight. With so many newcomers, Wyoming was named a U.S. territory in 1868. Cheyenne became the new territory's capital city.

Along with Wyoming's railroads came sportsmen who wanted to hunt bison. Some hunters shot their guns into bison herds right from the windows of moving trains. Most of these hunters did not want the bison's meat or hides. They killed the animals for sport. By the late 1800s, millions of bison had been killed.

Railroad workers built temporary wooden bridges *(at right)* for trains to use while permanent stone bridges were being put in place *(at left)*.

31

Ranchers burned a special mark, or brand, into the hides of cattle to tell their animals apart from others grazing freely on the open plains.

Settlers soon learned that beef cattle could live on Wyoming's plains almost as well as bison. In the 1870s and 1880s, cowboys drove huge herds from Texas to Wyoming, where the U.S. government offered free rangeland.

By 1886 about eight million cattle were grazing on the limited supply of grasses on the Great Plains. During the hot, dry summer of that year, very little grass grew. Thousands of already hungry cattle did not survive the severe winter that followed. Some ranchers lost so many cattle that they went out of business altogether.

In 1888 the Territory of Wyoming had about 62,000 residents—enough to ask the U.S. government for statehood. But some Wyomingites wondered if the government would accept their **constitution,** or set of written laws. Wyoming's state constitution granted women the right to vote—a right that women in other states did not yet have.

Many of Wyoming's residents didn't want to join the Union unless women could vote. They thought that allowing women the right to vote would be a good way to attract more people to Wyoming. After much discussion, the U.S. government approved the constitution, and on July 10, 1890, Wyoming became the 44th state.

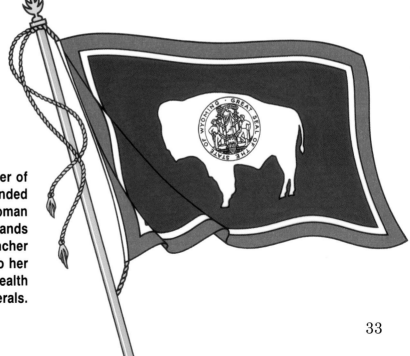

The buffalo in the center of Wyoming's state flag is branded with the state seal. The woman in the center of the seal stands for women's rights. The rancher at her left and the miner to her right symbolize Wyoming's wealth from cattle and minerals.

A blast of steam shoots out of a geyser in Yellowstone National Park.

In the early 1890s, workers drilled Wyoming's first oil wells and built an oil refinery in Casper to process the crude, or unprocessed, oil. Several years later, in 1912, a huge oil discovery near Casper gave the state's oil industry a big boost. Wyoming's role as a major oil producer had begun. Many people rushed to the state to take jobs drilling oil. Others found work in refineries where the crude oil was made into products such as kerosene and gasoline.

The gasoline was used to fuel the nation's first cars, and many vacationers began to drive to Wyoming. People came to the state from all over the world to see natural wonders such as the hot-water **geysers** in Yellowstone National Park.

Rodeo Cowgirls

Rodeo was one of the first sports in which women competed professionally. Cheyenne's famous Frontier Days, a rodeo held each year since 1897, opened competition to women in 1904. Cowgirls—such as Mabel Strickland *(left)* and Wyoming's Prairie Rose Henderson *(bottom)*—were famous for riding bucking broncos. Others pleased the crowds by roping horses and steers and performing fancy roping stunts *(right)*.

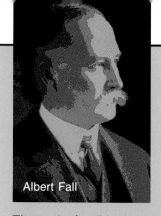
Albert Fall

The Teapot Dome Scandal

The nation's oil industry grew rapidly in the early 1900s, after cars were first built. Gasoline, an oil product, fueled the new autos. The U.S. government realized that gas also could fuel the ships of the U.S. Navy.

To make sure the navy would have enough oil for its ships, the U.S. government took control of three western oil fields. The oil at these sites would be saved for the navy's future use. One of these sites was the Teapot Dome oil field near Casper, Wyoming.

But some businesspeople wanted their companies to have the right to pump the oil and sell it right away. In 1922 Edward Doheny and Harry Sinclair, two rich oil executives, made a secret deal with a high-ranking government official named Albert Fall. He arranged for the two men's companies to drill for oil at two of the government's oil fields, including Teapot Dome. In exchange Fall accepted payments and livestock totaling about $400,000.

At first no one knew of the illegal arrangement. But word soon leaked out, and in 1922 the U.S. Senate began investigations, which led to several trials. The process of uncovering the truth took years. Finally in 1929, Fall was found guilty of accepting illegal payments and was sentenced to jail and had to pay a large fine. Doheny and Sinclair were ordered to pay millions of dollars to the government, and Sinclair was sent to jail for six months.

Harry Sinclair

Many tourists stopped coming to Wyoming after 1929, when an economic slump called the Great Depression began. Throughout the nation, banks failed, businesses closed, and many people lost their jobs. At first Wyoming's economy continued to benefit from increasing oil production. But by 1933, one out of every five people in Wyoming was out of work.

Lack of rain caused more problems for the state during the 1930s. Dams had been built across rivers to hold back water, which collected in large pools behind the dams. The water was needed for **irrigation**—the process of channeling water to dry farmland. But a drought, or long dry spell, dried up some of the rivers that once fed irrigation ditches. Crops grew poorly, and without rain, so did grass. Cattle and sheep that could not find enough to eat starved to death.

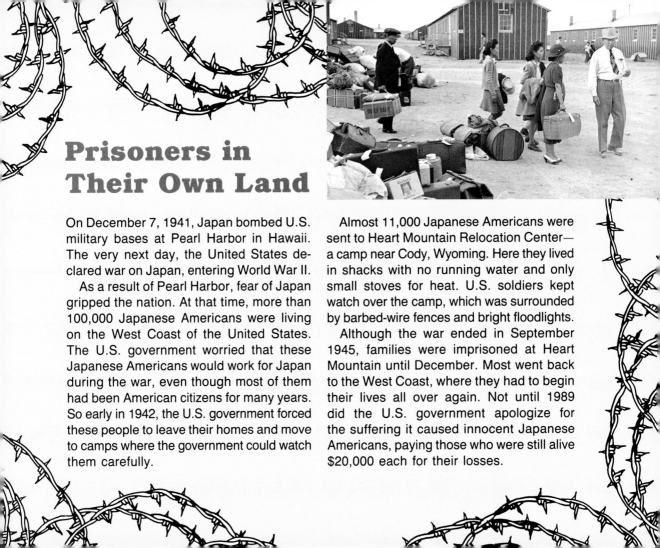

Prisoners in Their Own Land

On December 7, 1941, Japan bombed U.S. military bases at Pearl Harbor in Hawaii. The very next day, the United States declared war on Japan, entering World War II.

As a result of Pearl Harbor, fear of Japan gripped the nation. At that time, more than 100,000 Japanese Americans were living on the West Coast of the United States. The U.S. government worried that these Japanese Americans would work for Japan during the war, even though most of them had been American citizens for many years. So early in 1942, the U.S. government forced these people to leave their homes and move to camps where the government could watch them carefully.

Almost 11,000 Japanese Americans were sent to Heart Mountain Relocation Center— a camp near Cody, Wyoming. Here they lived in shacks with no running water and only small stoves for heat. U.S. soldiers kept watch over the camp, which was surrounded by barbed-wire fences and bright floodlights.

Although the war ended in September 1945, families were imprisoned at Heart Mountain until December. Most went back to the West Coast, where they had to begin their lives all over again. Not until 1989 did the U.S. government apologize for the suffering it caused innocent Japanese Americans, paying those who were still alive $20,000 each for their losses.

When the United States entered World War II in 1941, Wyoming's economy, along with the nation's, finally began to improve. During the war, the U.S. government bought much of the state's beef to feed the nation's soldiers. And Wyoming's supplies of oil and coal were needed to fuel the military's ships and tanks.

After the war ended in 1945, Wyoming's oil and coal industries grew even more. These fuels were used to help meet the nation's increasing demands for gasoline and electricity. In the 1970s, thousands of people came from other states looking for work in Wyoming's mines and oil fields. Between 1970 and 1980, Wyoming's population increased by more than 100,000 people.

In the 1980s, the nation found cheaper sources of energy in other countries. As a result, Wyoming's mining companies lost a lot of business. Thousands of people lost their jobs and left the state.

The people of Wyoming want to become less dependent on the changing demand for oil and coal New businesses, including some that make computer equipment, are starting up in the state. The tourists who flock to see Wyoming's natural wonders continue to be important to the state's economy as well.

9,000 B.C. Ancient hunters come to Wyoming

A.D. 1700 Plains Indians live throughout much of Wyoming

1803 Louisiana Purchase

1825 Trappers gather for the first time at Green River

1834 Fort William is built

1868 Wyoming becomes a U.S. territory

But even the state's natural wonders face risks. In the summer of 1988, forest fires swept through Yellowstone National Park. Before autumn snows finally put out the fires, almost half of the park had burned.

By the next spring, flowers and grass were already sprouting again on the scorched land. Vacationers came to photograph the park coming back to life. Wyomingites know that, like the park, they can survive hard times too.

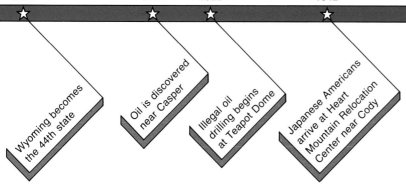

1890 — Wyoming becomes the 44th state

1912 — Oil is discovered near Casper

1922 — Illegal oil drilling begins at Teapot Dome

1942 — Japanese Americans arrive at Heart Mountain Relocation Center near Cody

1988 — Forest fires burn much of Yellowstone National Park

Although the Yellowstone fires of 1988 burned almost half the park, more wildflowers than usual bloomed the next spring.

41

Living and Working in Wyoming

Nowadays some of Wyoming's cowboys ride jeeps instead of horses for cattle roundups. But they are back in the saddle for the state's many rodeos. More than 8,000 ranches and farms and close to 100 yearly rodeos have earned Wyoming its unofficial nickname—the Cowboy State.

Many of Wyoming's 453,588 residents are descendants of the state's first European ranchers and farmers. In all, about 94 percent of Wyomingites are white. Many of the 3,600 African Americans in Wyoming can trace their roots to black soldiers who served at Wyoming's frontier forts in the 1800s. And many of the Latinos and Asian Americans who live in the state are descendants of the early Union Pacific Railroad workers.

Young dancers at a powwow wear beadwork and traditional costumes.

Nearly 10,000 Native Americans live in Wyoming, making up about 2 percent of the population. Around half of these Indians live and work on the Wind River Indian Reservation in western Wyoming. Each summer the Shoshone and Arapaho hold powwows, sun dances, and other traditional celebrations on the reservation.

Wyoming has fewer people than any other state in the country. More than half of the state's residents live in small cities or towns. The two largest cities, Cheyenne (the capital) and Casper, each have fewer than 60,000 people. Laramie, the state's third largest city, is home to just under 27,000 residents. Road signs in some towns announce populations of only 20, 15, or even as few as 5 people.

No matter where they live, the people of the Cowboy State are proud of their heritage. History buffs can walk in the pioneers' wagon ruts at Oregon Trail Ruts National Historic Landmark near Guernsey. Museums in Cheyenne, Cody, and Riverton specialize in Plains Indian history and artwork. The Whitney Gallery of Western Art in Cody displays the original works of many historic western artists, such as Frederic Remington and Charles M. Russell.

Crab apple trees blossom outside the state capitol building in Cheyenne.

Jackson's many art festivals draw visitors to the Tetons.

Cowboys ride bulls at rodeos across the state.

Current artists exhibit their work at the annual Jackson Hole Fall Arts Festival in Jackson. Each summer, nearby Teton Village hosts well-known classical musicians at the Grand Teton Music Festival. Music festivals throughout the state offer bluegrass, folk, and cowboy music, as well as polka and jazz. Western melodramas, in which players act out dramatic historical plots, draw tourists to many towns.

The Cowboy State's many rodeos are also popular. In Cody a rodeo takes place every night from June through August. Cheyenne's Frontier Days lasts for 10 days each July. At this well-known event, cowboys from across the nation rope steers and ride bucking broncos and bulls for cash prizes.

47

White-water rafting is a popular outdoor activity in Wyoming.

Wyoming's natural wonders also draw tourists to the state. Each year more than five million people visit Wyoming and spend about $1.5 billion. The most popular outdoor areas are Yellowstone and Grand Teton national parks. Yellowstone's famous Old Faithful geyser shoots more than 5,000 gallons (18,935 liters) of steaming hot water into the air about every 70 minutes. In the Tetons, Jackson Hole is a popular winter ski resort area.

Many hotel clerks and park rangers help Wyoming's tourists

to enjoy their stay. These workers have what are called service jobs. Service workers in Wyoming also buy and sell houses and land. Others work as teachers, doctors, lawyers, and cooks. About 700 people have jobs with the U.S. government at the Francis E. Warren Air Force Base in Cheyenne.

Many service workers in Casper and Cheyenne have jobs in banks and stores. Railroad workers help transport the state's minerals and farm products to customers all across the United States. Altogether about three out of four working Wyomingites have service jobs, helping other people or businesses.

The Union Pacific, Wyoming's first railroad, still provides jobs for many of the state's residents.

49

An oil-drilling rig pumps oil from deep underground.

Throughout the state, most people pay very close attention to the world's demand for oil, coal, natural gas, and other minerals. With large supplies of these fuels, Wyoming is among the top 10 mining states in the country. About 1 in 12 workers has a job in the mining industry, which earns the state more than $800 million each year.

Nearly 1 out of every 17 jobholders in Wyoming works in agriculture, which includes ranching and farming. Most ranches in Wyoming are about 4,000 acres (1,620 hectares), but some are much bigger. Many of Wyoming's sheep and cattle ranchers rent some of their grazing lands from the U.S. government, which owns about half the land in the state.

Wyoming's farmers raise nearly one million sheep each year.

With plenty of rich grazing land, livestock do well in Wyoming. But crops need a little extra help. The state has a short growing season and less precipitation than most other states. But with irrigation, crops can grow in most parts of the state. Wyoming's major crops include hay, wheat, and barley. In some areas, farmers also grow sugar beets and beans such as great northerns and pintos. Every year agriculture earns Wyoming about $200 million.

51

Some lumberjacks in Wyoming's forests use horses *(below)* to haul freshly cut logs. The wood is eventually transported to mills *(right)* to be made into lumber and other wood products.

Workers in the state's factories and processing plants know their jobs depend on Wyoming's crops and natural resources. Refinery workers in Cheyenne, Casper, and Sinclair process crude oil. Laborers in other factories make products such as farm equipment and chemical fertilizers for crops.

Food processors in north central Wyoming make sugar from sugar beets grown in the area. And some of the logs from the state's forests are cut into boards at sawmills in Cheyenne and Laramie or made into pulp for paper at other plants. Altogether about 1 out of every 25 workers in Wyoming has a manufacturing job. Whether they are miners, ranchers, factory workers, teachers, or salesclerks, Wyomingites are proud of the contribution they make to their state.

Protecting the Environment

Wyoming earns almost $1 billion a year from mining the state's rich supply of minerals. One of the most valuable and abundant of these minerals is coal. In fact, Wyoming produces almost 200 million tons (181 million metric tons) of coal a year—more than any other state in the nation. The coal is shipped to 5 different countries and 22 states, where most of it is burned at power plants to produce electricity.

Much of Wyoming's coal is mined in the Powder River Basin in the northeastern part of the state. The coal from this area contains less sulfur than coal from other regions, so it's in high demand. With less sulfur, the coal burns more cleanly and creates less air pollution.

Wyoming's coal is shipped by rail *(above)* to power plants *(left)* all over the country.

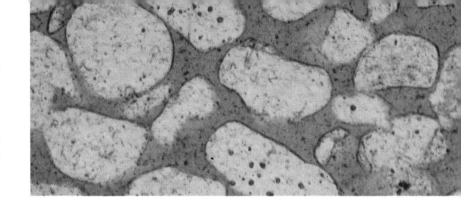

Many kinds of rocks hold groundwater. Photographed at 46 times its actual size, this piece of sandstone shows the large spaces between the grains of the rock where water is stored.

Burning coal from the Powder River Basin may help decrease air pollution. But coal mining also affects another natural resource—**groundwater**. This water, which lies under the earth's surface, is naturally stored in **aquifers,** or underground layers of rock. Many of Wyoming's residents worry that coal mining uses up too much of the state's groundwater.

Many of the state's aquifers provide an important source of clean, fresh drinking water for homes and businesses. Some of the aquifers contain water with a lot of iron, calcium, magnesium, and salt. These minerals make the water unsafe for people to drink. But farmers and ranchers can still use it for irrigating crops or for their livestock to drink.

In the Powder River Basin, the layers of coal serve as aquifers.

...oming has about **30** open-pit coal mines, such as this one in southwestern Wyoming.

Before miners dig up the coal, they first pump out water from the coal aquifers. Then, in a process called strip mining, huge bulldozers remove all the topsoil, plants, and rocky materials that cover the coal bed, creating a giant pit. Workers use explosives to blast the exposed coal bed. This breaks up the coal so that it can be easily s and hauled away.

To control the coal d by blasting, miners spray the pit with pumped from the c When still more water is pumped from aqui much deeper undergr

A front-er scoops c railroad c

Wy

Each year coal-mining companies pump out millions of gallons of water from aquifers. The mining companies eventually release the water into local rivers and streams. Over time water from these waterways and from precipitation seeps back into the ground, naturally recharging (refilling) aquifers. But recharging an aquifer takes many years, especially in areas such as the Powder River Basin that receive very little precipitation.

Wyomingites concerned about protecting their state's water resources have formed groups such as the Powder River Basin Resource Council and the Wyoming Outdoor Council. These groups print newsletters that help people understand the issues related to mining in their state. The groups also work to convince the state of Wyoming and the U.S. government to pass tougher environmental laws and to enforce the laws that already exist.

A law passed in 1977, for example, requires coal-mining companies to reclaim, or rebuild, the land they've mined. In this process, called **reclamation,** all of the rocky materials and soil that were removed are placed back into the pit after the coal is mined. Grass and trees are planted. Wells are dug to study the quality and quantity of groundwater in the area.

Companies reclaim coal pits when the mining job is finished.

Sometimes mining companies discover they've used up a source of water that ranchers and other residents depended on for their homes and businesses. Mining companies are required by law to find new sources of water to replace what has been lost. This may mean tapping an aquifer that is much farther away or deeper underground. These problems can take years to fix and can make the water costly to pump.

Many mining companies do an

excellent job of reclaiming the land they've mined. And some of the money that mining companies earn each year goes toward reclaiming mines that were dug and abandoned before the 1977 law was passed.

All Wyomingites can help protect groundwater. Residents can use less electricity, for example, so less coal will be needed to fuel electric power plants. And Wyomingites who think a mining company is breaking environmental laws can ask Wyoming's Department of Environmental Quality in Cheyenne to investigate. By working together, Wyomingites can help their state protect and conserve groundwater while providing the coal that the nation requires.

A biologist checks to see how well plants are growing on reclaimed land.

61

Wyoming's Famous People

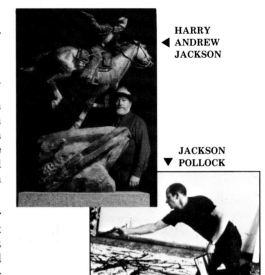

HARRY
◄ ANDREW
JACKSON

JACKSON
▼ POLLOCK

Harry Andrew Jackson (born 1924), a sculptor and painter, can trace his interest in Western subjects to his youth. When Jackson was 14, he ran away to Wyoming and worked as a ranch hand. The artist is best known for his painted bronze sculptures of figures such as movie star John Wayne and Sacagawea, a Shoshone Indian guide of the 1800s. Jackson lives in Cody.

Jackson Pollock (1912–1956) was a painter born on a ranch near Cody. Considered a leader in abstract expressionist art, Pollock became famous for his painting technique. The artist would first put a canvas on the floor and then use a stick or trowel—instead of a brush—to drip paint onto the canvas, forming unpredictable patterns.

◄ JOE
ALEXANDER

MIKE
DEVEREAUX ▼

ATHLETES

Joe Alexander (born 1943) is a world-champion rodeo star. Born in Jackson, Alexander won the professional rodeo world championship title in bareback bronco riding each year from 1971 to 1975. He was elected to the ProRodeo Hall of Fame in 1979.

Mike Devereaux (born 1963) is an outfielder for the Baltimore Orioles baseball team. In 1992 Devereaux batted in 107 runs, becoming the first Oriole in 12 years to drive in 100 or more runs in a season. Devereaux is from Casper.

62

Boyd H. Dowler (born 1937), from Cheyenne, was a leading receiver for the Green Bay Packers in the 1960s. During his 11-year professional career, he caught 449 passes for a total of 6,894 yards (6,304 m) and scored 39 touchdowns. Dowler was named to the Green Bay Packers Hall of Fame in 1978.

BUSINESS LEADERS

Nancy Curtis (born 1947) is a rancher and book publisher in Glendo, Wyoming. In 1984 she founded Wyoming's first book publishing company—High Plains Press, which puts out books about Wyoming and other parts of the western United States.

Leonard S. Hobbs (1896–1977) was originally from Carbon, Wyoming. In 1952 he created an engine that could thrust a fighter plane forward at nearly 755 miles (1,215 km) per hour. This work made passenger jet travel possible.

▲ BOYD H. DOWLER

NANCY CURTIS ▶

◀ CURT GOWDY

CHRIS LEDOUX ▶

ENTERTAINERS

Curt Gowdy (born 1919), a sportscaster from Green River, Wyoming, hosted a TV show called "American Sportsman." Starting in the 1960s, the show ran for almost 20 years. In 1984 Gowdy was elected to the Baseball Hall of Fame.

Chris LeDoux (born 1948) is a country singer and songwriter, rancher, and rodeo champion who moved to Cheyenne as a teenager. In 1976 he won the world championship title in bareback bronco riding at the National Finals Rodeo. LeDoux's songs include "I've Got to Be a Rodeo Man" and "Cadillac Ranch."

James P. Beckwourth (1798–1867?) was an African American fur trapper, guide, and scout. Born in Virginia, Beckwourth explored much of Wyoming for the Rocky Mountain Fur Company in the 1820s. His autobiography, *Life and Adventures of James P. Beckwourth,* describes his life as a mountain man.

James Bridger (1804–1881) was a fur trapper and Rocky Mountain explorer from Virginia who became one of the best-known mountain men in the country. In 1838 he built Fort Bridger, which became a major trading post in southwestern Wyoming for pioneers heading west.

◄ JAMES P. BECKWOURTH

JAMES BRIDGER ►

▼ RED CLOUD

WASHAKIE ▲

NATIVE AMERICAN LEADERS

Red Cloud (Makhpíya-Lúta) (1822–1909), born in Nebraska, was an Oglala Sioux leader. In the 1860s, he and his followers attacked wagon trains in an effort to close the Bozeman Trail—a pioneer trail that crossed Sioux hunting grounds in northeastern Wyoming. In 1868 the U.S. government signed a treaty agreeing to close the trail. Red Cloud is sometimes referred to as the only Native American to ever win a war against the U.S. government.

Washakie (1804?–1900) was the leader of the Eastern Shoshone Indians. Born in Montana, he spent much of his life in Wyoming, where he and his people were helpful to the U.S. Army and to pioneers heading west in the mid-1800s. At his death, Washakie became the first Native American leader to be buried with U.S. military honors.

Richard Cheney (born 1941) moved to Casper as a child. He was in his sixth term as a U.S. congressman from Wyoming when President George Bush appointed him secretary of defense. Cheney served in that role from 1989 to 1992.

Esther Hobart Morris (1814–1902) moved to South Pass City, Wyoming, in 1869. Less than a year later, the governor of the Territory of Wyoming appointed her to be a justice of the peace, making Morris the nation's first woman judge.

Nellie Tayloe Ross (1876–1977), the nation's first female governor, moved to Cheyenne with her husband in 1902. In 1925 she was elected to complete her husband's term as governor of Wyoming after he died in office. In 1933 Ross went on to become the first female director of the U.S. Mint.

◀ RICHARD CHENEY

▲ NELLIE ROSS

◀ ESTHER MORRIS

◀ PATRICIA MACLACHLAN

PEGGY SIMPSON ▶ CURRY

WRITERS

Peggy Simpson Curry (1911–1987), born in Scotland, eventually settled in Casper. Her books include *Red Wind of Wyoming* and a novel for young readers called *A Shield of Clover*.

Patricia MacLachlan (born 1938), an author of children's books, was born in Cheyenne. In 1986 she won a Newbery Medal for her book *Sarah, Plain and Tall*, which was made into a television movie in 1991.

Elinore Pruitt Stewart (1878–1935) owned a ranch near Burntfork, Wyoming. She wrote about her life in *Letters of a Woman Homesteader*, which was made into a movie in 1979.

65

Facts-at-a-Glance ━━━━━

Nickname: Equality State
Song: "Wyoming"
Motto: Equal Rights
Flower: Indian paintbrush
Tree: cottonwood
Bird: meadowlark

Population: 453,588*
Rank in population, nationwide: 50th
Area: 97,818 sq mi (253,349 sq km)
Rank in area, nationwide: 10th
Date and ranking of statehood:
   July 10, 1890, the 44th state
Capital: Cheyenne
Major cities (and populations*):
   Cheyenne (50,008), Casper (46,742), Laramie
   (26,687), Rock Springs (19,050),
   Sheridan (13,900)
U.S. senators: 2
U.S. representatives: 1
Electoral votes: 3

Places to visit: Red Desert near Wamsutter, Flaming Gorge National Recreation Area near Green River, Fort Laramie National Historic Site near Fort Laramie, Register Cliff near Guernsey, Buffalo Bill Historical Center in Cody, Indian Heritage Center near Riverton

Annual events: Horse-drawn sleigh races in Jackson (Jan.), Frontier Days in Cheyenne (July), Grand Teton Music Festival in Teton Village (July and August), Wyoming State Fair in Douglas (August), Cowboy Days in Evanston (Sept.)

*1990 census

66

Average January temperature: 19° F (–7° C)　　**Average July temperature:** 67° F (20° C)

Natural resources: coal, petroleum, natural gas, trona, bentonite, agate, jade, gold, gypsum, limestone, zeolites, forests, grazing land

Agricultural products: cattle, milk, sheep, wool, alfalfa, hay, barley, wheat, oats, sugar beets, corn, beans, potatoes

Manufactured goods: fertilizer and other chemicals, petroleum products, machinery, newspapers and other printed materials, wood products

ENDANGERED AND THREATENED SPECIES
Mammals—grizzly bear, brown bear, fisher, least weasel, wolverine, wood bison, gray wolf, black-footed ferret
Birds—piping plover, brown pelican, wood stork, bald eagle, peregrine falcon, whooping crane
Fish—Colorado river squawfish, golden trout, greenback cutthroat trout, humpback chub, bonytail, June sucker, Kendall warm springs dace
Plants—stemless beardtongue, woolrush, Laramie false sagebrush, small rockcress, livid sedge, woolly fleabane, dwarf scouring rush

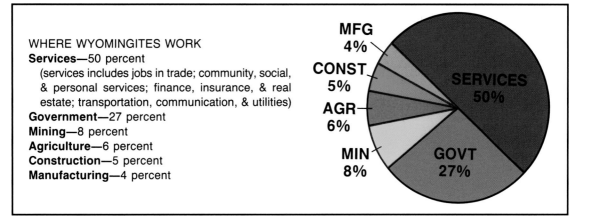

WHERE WYOMINGITES WORK
Services—50 percent
　(services includes jobs in trade; community, social, & personal services; finance, insurance, & real estate; transportation, communication, & utilities)
Government—27 percent
Mining—8 percent
Agriculture—6 percent
Construction—5 percent
Manufacturing—4 percent

MFG 4%
CONST 5%
AGR 6%
MIN 8%
SERVICES 50%
GOVT 27%

67

Arapaho (uh-RAP-uh-hoh)

Cheyenne (shy-AN)

Cody (KOH-dee)

Guernsey (GURN-zee)

Lakota (luh-KOH-tuh)

Laramie (LEHR-uh-mee)

Platte (PLAT)

Shoshone (shuh-SHOHN)

Sioux (SOO)

Teton (TEE-tahn)

Glossary

aquifer An underground layer of rock, sand, or gravel containing water that can be drawn out for use above ground.

basin A bowl-shaped region. Also, all the land drained by a river and its branches.

constitution The system of basic laws or rules of a government, society, or organization. The document in which these laws or rules are written.

continental divide A line of elevated land that determines the direction the rivers of a continent flow. In North America, the line is sometimes called the Great Divide. The Rocky Mountains mark the North American divide, separating rivers that flow east from those that flow west.

geyser An underground spring heated by very hot rocks. The spring periodically throws a jet of hot water and steam into the air through an opening in the ground.

groundwater Water that lies beneath the earth's surface. The water comes from rain and snow that seep through soil into the cracks and other openings in rocks. Groundwater supplies wells and springs.

immigrant A person who moves into a foreign country and settles there.

irrigation A method of watering land by directing water through canals, ditches, pipes, or sprinklers.

plateau A large, relatively flat area that stands above the surrounding land.

precipitation Rain, snow, and other forms of moisture that fall to earth.

reclamation The process of rebuilding land and making it usable again for plants, animals, or people.

reservation Public land set aside by the government to be used by Native Americans.

treaty An agreement between two or more groups, usually having to do with peace or trade.

Index ▰▰▰▰▰

Acknowledgments:

Maryland Cartographics, pp. 2, 10; WY Division of Tourism, pp. 2–3, 50; Robert Tyszka, pp. 6, 11, 26, 49, 57; Jack Lindstrom, p. 7; Tom Dietrich, pp. 8 (right), 45, 47, 48, 52–53; © Adam Jones, pp. 8 (left), 17 (lower right); Jeff Vanuga, pp. 9, 12, 15, 17 (upper right), 25 (inset), 42, 44, 51, 52, 71; Robert Czarnomski, pp. 13, 43; Kent & Donna Dannen, pp. 14, 16; J. Loomis / NE Stock Photo, p. 17; IPS, pp. 19, 20; WY State Museum, pp. 21, 32, 34, 35 (right), 36–37, 65 (top right); Denver Public Library, Western History Dept., pp. 23, 25, 65 (top center); American Heritage Center, Univ. of WY, pp. 27, 35 (left and center), 37; Univ. of MI Museum of Art, Bequest of Henry C. Lewis, 1895.80, p. 29; Oakland Museum History Dept., pp. 30–31; Clara Olsen Collection, neg. #22589, NM State Records Center & Archives, p. 36; Buffalo Bill Historical Center, Cody, WY, Jack Richard Collection, p. 38; Domenica Di Piazza, p. 41; C. W. Biedel, M.D. / Laatsch-Hupp Photo, p. 46; © Scott T. Smith, pp. 54–55, 55, 58, 60, 61; American Assoc. of Petroleum Geologists, p. 56; Marcello Bertoni, p. 62 (top left); Jackson Pollock Papers, Archives of American Art, Smithsonian Institution, p. 62 (top right); PRCA Photo, p. 62 (bottom left); Mort Tadder / Baltimore Orioles, p. 62 (bottom right); Green Bay Packers, p. 63 (top left); Dove Studio, p. 63 (top right); Curt Gowdy, p. 63 (bottom left); Butch Adams, p. 63 (bottom right); UT State Historical Society, p. 64 (top right and left); *Dictionary of American Portraits*, p. 64 (bottom right); Smithsonian Institution National Anthropological Archives, Bureau of American Ethnology Collection, p. 64 (bottom left); DOD Photo, p. 65 (top left); Anne MacLachlan, p. 65 (bottom left); Casper College Library, p. 65 (bottom right); Jean Matheny, p. 66; Jerry Hennen, p. 69.